KIRA VELIKANOVA

66 Poems by AI and Human

Poems on Love and Nature by Kira Velikanova in the synergy with AI

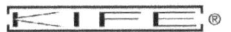

Contents

1

Love's First Glance

A glance, love blooms.
  Eyes connect, hearts soar.
  Lips speak, minds merge.
  Souls ignite, passion burns.

2

Nature's Beauty

Breathtaking views, grand,
  Nature's beauty, enchant,
  Artwork by divine hand,
  A sight to understand.

3

A Love Beyond Compare

Intense passion, pure,
  A love beyond compare,
  Heart and soul entwine,
  A bond to forever shine.

4

Endless Possibilities

Sky limitless, wide,
Worlds to explore, ride,
Endless possibilities, clear,
Dreams to chase, near.

5

Our Love Story

From first glance,
  To a timeless romance,
  Adventures shared, bold,
  Our love story, unfold.

Delicate Emotions

Fragile hearts, true,
Emotions raw, new,
Tenderness unfurled,
Delicate love world.

7

The Joy of Spring

Renewal, hope, love,
  Nature's canvas, abuzz,
  Warmth, growth, fresh start,
  The joy of spring, heart.

8

Breathtaking Views

Views that steal breath,
   A sight beyond depth,
   Nature's beauty, immense,
   Breathtaking, intense.

A Heart Full of Love

Heart filled with love,
  Compassionate, pure dove,
  Overflowing emotions, bold,
  A heart full of love, unfold.

10

My Beloved Nature

In nature's embrace,
  I find peace, grace,
  Soulful connection, pure,
  My beloved nature, allure.

11

The Magic of Love

Mystery, enchantment, spell,
　Love's magic, can't tell,
　Unfathomable bond, strong,
　The magic of love, lifelong.

12

The Warmth of The Sun

Golden rays, pure heat,
  Nature's warmth, complete,
  Light to guide, hold,
  The warmth of the sun, bold.

13

A Love that Lasts

Eternal flame, pure,
A love that forever endures,
Heart and soul, entwine,
A love that lasts, divine.

14

Endless Beauty

Nature's endless beauty, grand,
A sight beyond, understand,
A world of pure delight,
Endless beauty in sight.

15

The Sweetness of Life

Life's sweetness, pure bliss,
   Moments treasured, not miss,
   Smiles, laughter, love,
   The sweetness of life, dove.

16

A Love Beyond Words

Deeper than words,
  A love that forever lasts,
  Heart and soul entwine,
  A bond that's divine.

17

The Calm of The Sea

Sea's calm, peaceful, pure,
   Rhythmic waves, heart's cure,
   Soothing, serene, calm,
   The calm of the sea, balm.

18

The Essence of Love

Heart's pure essence,
  Soul's connection, immense,
  Emotions raw, new,
  The essence of love, true.

19

Beautiful Horizons

A view to cherish,
   A sight to nourish,
   Nature's wonder, grand,
   Beautiful horizons, expand.

20

A Garden of Love

Garden of love, pure,
  Blossoming, secure,
    Heart and soul, entwine,
    A love that's divine.

21

The Sweetness of a Kiss

A kiss, pure bliss,
  Soulful connection, amiss,
  Heartbeats skip, bold,
  The sweetness of a kiss, hold.

22

The Miracle of Love

Healing hearts with tenderness.
  Magic in the mundane.
  Divine intervention prevails.
  Transforming all it touches.

23

A Garden of Love

Blossoming with passion's fire,
Evergreen with love's desire,
Blooming with sweetest devotion,
Flourishing with tender emotion.

24

A Tranquility of a Stream

Flowing peacefully and gently,
Reflecting nature's serenity,
Soothing whispers of calmness,
A tranquil escape from darkness.

25

Love's Miracle, Divine Intervention

Heart opened, love's found.
Divine timing, perfect match.
Soulmates, fate intervened.
Miracle, love's magic.

26

Peace of the Forest

Nature's embrace, soothing calm.
Trees whisper, troubles fade.
Quiet serenity, tranquil refuge.
Forest's peace, heals all.

27

Love's Spark

Flames dance, love's blaze.
  Heart's desire, fiery passion.
  Electric chemistry, sparks fly.
  Love ignited, passion aflame.

28

Grace of Nature's Embrace

Nature's beauty, grace surrounds.
  Gentle breeze, calming touch.
  Sun's warmth, nature's embrace.
  Graceful nature, heals all.

29

Love Like No Other

Unique connection, soulmates found.
  Deeper love, beyond compare.
  Heart and soul, intertwined.
  Love like no other, pure bliss.

30

Freedom of a Butterfly

Graceful flutter, wings spread.
  Fragile beauty, free spirit.
  Butterfly's freedom, inspires hope.
  Hopeful journey, life's beauty.

31

Power of Love

Heart awakened, life transformed.
  Love's power, heals all wounds.
  Transformative love, changes everything.
  Powerful love, conquers all.

32

Serenity of the Ocean

Gentle waves, peaceful calm.
   Ocean's rhythm, soothes the soul.
   Sea breeze, tranquil refuge.
   Serenity of the ocean, heals all.

33

Beauty of the Sunset

Sun's golden kiss, painted sky.
  Colorful canvas, breathtaking view.
  Peaceful moment, tranquil delight.
  Beauty of the sunset, pure joy.

34

Love. Unique and Special

Heart's treasure, love's gift.
  Soulmate's bond, rare connection.
  Unique love, beyond compare.
  Special love, meant to be.

35

Comfort of a Rose

Delicate petals, soft touch.
  Aroma sweet, comforting embrace.
  Rose's comfort, eases pain.
  Nature's gift, heals all.

36

Mystery of Love's Allure

Enigmatic pull, love's mystery.
  Unexplainable attraction, heart's desire.
  Magnetic connection, soulmates found.
  Mystery of love's allure, fate's design.

37

Majesty of Mountains

Mountain's majesty, towering heights.
    Love elevated, soaring heights.
    Soul's journey, climbing peaks.
    Majesty of mountains, love's magnificence.

38

Nature's Art

Nature's canvas, beauty expressed.
  Colorful palette, exquisite art.
  Masterpiece of creation, nature's art.
  Beauty expressed, beyond compare.

39

Love of My Dreams

Heart's desire, love's dream.
  Soulmate found, life's treasure.
  Dreams fulfilled, love's bliss.
  Love of my dreams, destiny's call.

40

Calm of a Lake

Still waters, peaceful calm.
  Tranquil setting, nature's gift.
  Serenity of the lake, soothes the soul.
  Calm of the lake, restores all.

41

Our Love

Soul's connection, heart's bond.
Unbreakable tie, love's unity.
Two hearts, beat as one.
Love that unites us, eternal love.

42

Grace of a Swan

Swan's grace, pure beauty.
  Heart's purity, love's essence.
  Majestic creature, symbol of love.
  Grace of a swan, love's purity revealed.

43

Wonder of Love's Journey

Heart's adventure, love's journey.
  Unexpected turns, twists and bends.
  Joyful moments, love's reward.
  Wonder of love's journey, life's treasure.

44

Magnificence of a Rainbow

Colorful spectrum, rainbow's grace.
   Love's magic, beauty expressed.
   Healing power, love's embrace.
   Magnificence of a rainbow, love's spectrum revealed.

45

Love

Satisfies the heart's hunger,
   Fuels life's passions,
   Fosters growth and strength,
   Sustains us through hardship.

46

Joy of a Bird's Song

Melodic and uplifting,
   Nature's sweet symphony,
   Filling hearts with gladness,
   A reminder of hope.

Beauty of a Starry Night

Awe-inspiring wonder,
    Glimmering in the dark,
    A peaceful respite,
    An enchanting escape.

48

Magic of Love's Touch

A spark that ignites,
An electric connection,
A feeling of completeness,
A moment of pure bliss.

49

Serenity of a Meadow

A tranquil oasis,
   A peaceful refuge,
   A place to find calm,
   And rest for the soul.

50

Strength of Love's Embrace

A powerful force,
   A source of comfort,
   A shelter from the storm,
   A bond that endures.

51

Inspiration of Nature's Beauty

A wellspring of creativity,
   An artist's palette of hues,
   A muse that never fades,
   A source of infinite wonder.

52

Love that Grows

A tender sprout emerging,
  A blossom opening wide,
  A tree that stretches skyward,
  A garden bursting with life.

Tranquility of a Stream

A gentle flowing rhythm,
   A soothing melody of water,
   A calming presence,
   A balm for the mind.

54

Allure of Love's Charm

A magnetic pull,
   An irresistible appeal,
   A captivating essence,
   A spellbinding attraction.

55

Majesty of a Thunderstorm

Nature's fierce power unleashed,
    An electrifying energy,
    A reminder of the might,
    That love can possess.

56

Beauty of a Dandelion

A simple flower,
   A symbol of resilience,
   A beauty in simplicity,
   A reminder of the extraordinary in the ordinary.

57

Love's Journey

A winding path,
    Full of twists and turns,
    Navigated with courage and faith,
    Leading to a treasure beyond compare.

58

Enchantment of a Forest

A mystical realm,
   Full of secrets and wonder,
   A verdant tapestry of life,
   A place of magic and mystery.

59

Splendor of Love's Radiance

A brilliant light shining,
   Illuminating the darkness,
   A beacon of hope
   A source of warmth and comfort.

Dance of a Butterfly

Graceful and vibrant,
Fluttering in the breeze,
A symbol of transformation,
A celebration of life's beauty.

61

Love that Inspires Us

A catalyst for change,
  A motivation to grow,
  A reason to strive,
  A light that never fades.

62

Miracle of a Rainbow

A colorful bridge of hope,
  Connecting sky and earth,
  A reminder of life's beauty,
  A blessing from above.

63

Wonder of Love's Mystery

A never-ending enigma,
   A puzzle to unravel,
   A journey of discovery,
   A riddle that captivates the soul.

64

Love that Heals

A soothing balm for pain,
  A gentle salve for scars,
  A source of renewal,
  A catalyst for growth.

65

Tranquility of a Garden

A peaceful haven,
   A place of rest and renewal,
   A bower of beauty,
   A sanctuary for the soul.

Beauty of a Promise

A commitment of the heart,
A vow to cherish and protect,
A pledge of forever love,
A promise of beauty and joy.

About the Author

Artist.
Passionate.
Curious.

You can connect with me on:

🔗 https://www.instagram.com/kiraivelikanova

www.ingramcontent.com/pod-product-compliance
Lightning Source LLC
Chambersburg PA
CBHW070457220526
45466CB00004B/1868